Dancing Ging

Story by Jacquie Kilkenny
Photography by Lindsay Edwards

One Saturday morning,
Riley said to Grandad,
"Please can we make
some gingerbread men today?"

"Yes, we can," laughed Grandad.
"I like eating gingerbread.
It's my favourite."

Grandad helped Riley
make the gingerbread.
Then they cut out six little men
and put them on a tray.

Riley put a mouth,
and two eyes and a nose
on all of them.

"Our gingerbread men
look very good," said Grandad.
"Now they are ready to be cooked."

Grandad put the tray in the oven.
"They won't take very long to cook,"
he said.

"Can we look at them, now?"
said Riley.

"Yes," said Grandad.

Riley got a surprise.
The gingerbread men
were getting bigger.

Riley looked in the oven again.

"Grandad!" he cried.

"The gingerbread men
are getting so big
they will fall off the tray.
It is too little for them."

"No, they won't fall off,"
laughed Grandad.

Grandad looked at his watch.

"Can you smell them cooking, Riley?"
he said.

Grandad opened the oven door.

"Stay over there, Riley," he said.

"It's time to take them out.

The tray will be hot."

Grandad took the tray from the oven and put it on the bench.

"Our gingerbread men
look like they are holding hands,"
laughed Riley.
"They are dancing in two little lines.
Can I eat one please, Grandad?"

"Mmm…mmm," smiled Riley.
"This is the best!
We will have to make
dancing gingerbread men, again."